Covenant Bible
Study Series

Jonah:
God's Global Reach

by
Paula Bowser

faithQuest
the trade imprint of Brethren Press
Elgin, Illinois

Covenant Bible Study Series

Jonah: God's Global Reach

Paula Bowser

Copyright © 1992 by *faithQuest*, the trade imprint of **Brethren Press**, 1451 Dundee Avenue, Elgin, IL 60120

Biblical quotations, unless otherwise noted, are from the New Revised Standard Version of the Bible, copyrighted 1989 by the Division of Christian Education, National Council of Churches, and are used by permission.

Cover Photo by D. Jeanene Tiner Photographcs, House Springs MO 63051
Cover design by Jeane Healy

Manufactured in the United States of America

Contents

Foreword

The book of Jonah begins with the Word of the Lord coming to the prophet—the usual beginning for an Old Testament prophetic story. But from that point on, this prophet's story is like no other. It reads like a quick-paced adventure story; it is filled with humor and irony; and the characters are sharply drawn—the petulant prophet, the desperate sailors, the repentant king, even a big fish!

This biblical story of Jonah is one that captivated our grandson several years ago. His favorite picture in a series drawn by an elementary-age church school class showed a huge whale, with a tiny Jonah standing upright in the gaping mouth. To Joseph, at four years of age, this picture captured his imagination, as well as the essence of the story of Jonah.

But what is an appropriate understanding of Jonah at age four or five is hardly adequate for adults. What is God's message for today's world, when fear and distrust, violence and war are so prevalent? What is the prophetic word to a people who too glibly categorize the "good guys" and "bad guys," the "Christian nations" and "evil empires"?

This study, *Jonah: God's Global Reach*, challenges us as Christians to confess our Jonah-like tendencies to run away, the Nineveh we believe unworthy of God's mercy, our unwillingness to recognize the magnitude of the Creator's love, and finally, to discover how very relevant the message of Jonah is for the 1990s.

This is a relational Bible study, designed for small group settings. As you begin your study, you will want to keep in mind the characteristics of relational Bible study, some of which differ from other types of Bible study.

It is important to remember that relational Bible study is anchored in covenantal history. God covenanted with people in Old Testament history, established a new covenant in Jesus Christ, and covenants with the church today.

Relational Bible study takes seriously corporate faith. As each person contributes to study, prayer, and work, the group becomes the real body of Christ. Each one's contribution is needed and important. "For just as the body is one and has many members, so it is with Christ.

. . . Now you are the body of Christ and individually members of it" (1 Cor. 12:12,17).

Relational Bible study helps both individuals and the group to claim the promise of the Spirit and the working of the Spirit. As one person testified, "In our commitment to one another and in our sharing, something happened. . . . We were woven together in love by the Master Weaver. It is something that can happen only when two or three or seven are gathered in God's name, and we know the promise of God's presence in our lives."

With these understandings of relational Bible study, you will want to give careful attention to these guidelines:

1. As a small group of learners, we gather around God's Word to discern its meaning for today.
2. The words, stories, and admonitions we find in scripture come alive for today, challenging and renewing us.
3. All persons are learners and all are leaders.
4. Each person will contribute to the study, sharing the meaning found in the scripture and helping to bring meaning to others.
5. We recognize each other's vulnerability as we share out of our own experience, and in sharing, we learn to trust others and to be trustworthy.

May your study of *Jonah: God's Global Reach* lead to deeper understandings of God's mercy and love, to be lived out in prophetic witness in God's world.

June Adams Gibble
Elgin, Illinois

1

Who's in Charge: God or Jonah?
The Book of Jonah

Preparation

1. Find a New Revised Standard Version of the Bible and look up the last 12 books of the Old Testament. These are called the minor (meaning shorter—not less significant) prophets.
2. Thumb through the minor prophets starting with Hosea and going through Malachi. Notice their short length, how they look on the page, and the dark, commanding tone in many of them. Make a mental note of recurring phrases and words such as "Woe!" or "The word of the Lord came to . . . " or "Hear this!" or "It shall come to pass . . ."
3. Pretend you are a child and that you have never heard of Jonah before. Read the book through in one sitting. As a first impression, what do you think is the theme or main idea of the book?

Understanding

Every single time I tell people that I am working on the book of Jonah I get smiles. And, along with a grin, there is often a nod and a knowing look. "Ah, Jonah!" friends say. All of them take the Bible very seriously, but when Jonah is mentioned they just smile. Perhaps, unconsciously, they are aware that there is something undeniably comic about the way the story is told.

First of all, the very notion of the word of the Lord going to Nineveh would have been a repulsive scandal to Israel when the book of Jonah was written. And the idea of Nineveh's total and radical repentance borders on farce. Beyond this is the personality of our hero.

Looking at Jonah reminds me of two things: looking at my own faults reflected in the actions of my children or looking in a mirror. Jonah is a caricature of all of us at our worst. More than anything he resembles a spoiled child. He whines about looking absurd to the Ninevites. He foolishly imagines that he can run away in a boat from his all-knowing Parent. Bluntly and honestly, with no apparent sense of shame, he declares his selfish wish that the Ninevites perish so he can salvage his reputation. He pouts over the withered bush. To the bitter end, as he leaves God's question hanging in stubborn silence, his rebelliousness and sheer selfishness are sorry reflections of our own childish ways. We can easily see these qualities in our own lives; and we often find excuses or explain them away. But in the man of God they are downright comic.

Another aspect that contributes to the humor of *Jonah* is the irony that strikes the reader again and again. Things keep turning out exactly the opposite from what one might expect. Not only does our hero refuse his commission, he goes as far as possible in the opposite direction. At sea, the heathen sailors (not the prophet of Israel) recognize the hand of God in the raging storm. In stark contrast to Jonah's disobedience and vengefulness, the sailors are ethically sensitive, throwing him overboard only as a last resort. Then, as if to add insult to injury, they offer a sacrifice and make vows to the God of the Hebrews.

Nineveh, too, delivers an ironic twist. Not only does Nineveh listen to Jonah, the people actually repent! After only eight words, the godless king of this pagan city understands the divine compassion. He sees at once that God's real desire is to save and not to destroy. Not Jonah! It has taken immense pressure on God's part just to get him to *go* to Nineveh in the first place. Then, far from being pleased by his unexpected success, he is furious! Mortified! Long after Nineveh's repentance, God has to patiently explain to Israel's prophet all about compassion. While Jonah can pity an inanimate plant, he cannot summon mercy for thousands of people. Irony and humor abound.

It's difficult to picture Jonah without smiling. We see him stomping off to Tarshish in a huff or draped in seaweed trying to pray. We imagine his physical state as he is coughed up on the beach, reeking of fish, or how he is sandblasted by the east wind, a wind he had hoped would demolish Nineveh. His words seem like the ravings of a child in a tantrum.

Yet for all of its humor, the message of Jonah is not funny in the least. The Jews who heard it would not have been amused. If you have ever been the focus of someone else's joke, you understand how such humor has the power to scold in a way that no serious comment can.

Often, pictures tell a story. Think about how quickly we turn to the cartoons in a newspaper or magazine. We may read the articles carefully at a later time, but it is the cartoonist who captures our attention first. We can't wait to hear what he or she will say. And we smile. But even as we do, we are burned by the truth. Clearly, this kind of humor has a point. And its message is a serious one.

The writer of Jonah tells his story as a tale. However, he refers to an actual person and a real city, giving the story an historical basis. (We will learn more about the son of Amittai in chapter two.) He speaks of a real city, not the Emerald City in Oz or Atlantis. He states flatly that God appointed the fish, the plant, and the wind. We need not decide—indeed we can never know for sure—if this book is a history or if the story of Jonah, like the story of the Prodigal Son, is partly or wholly a product of a great writer's imagination. Parables contain truth, although the truth they contain is not necessarily historical truth. It may be a satire that pokes fun while masquerading as history. It is quite possible that no one who heard this story when it was first told would have questioned its validity as a factual event in human history. After all, God is omnipotent. The Creator made the sea and everything in it: the wind, the storm, and all that grows. And if God wishes to use these things to accomplish a purpose, who are we to question and doubt?

But the original recipients of *Jonah* knew, as we do, that this is an unconventional history, to say the least. It is outrageous, shocking, even ludicrous. Leslie C. Allen notes that it is " . . . crammed with an accumulation of hair-raising and eye-popping phenomena, one after the other . . . " (*New International Commentary,* p. 176).

None of this would have been lost on the Jewish audience. They would have asked, "What does this writer mean to say?" not "Did this really happen?"

You can almost picture their excitement and surprise as they absorb the strange tale. They are intrigued at once by the name of Jonah (Jonah means "dove"), and they understand that this bird is a symbol of Israel. And they soon understand that the focus of the humor is none other than the Jewish nation and, in a deeper sense, themselves.

They would not have debated whether Jonah was a history. Rather, they would have been cut to the quick by its message. When you have been scalded, you do not waste time deciding whether it was steam or boiling water that burned. You immediately tend to the wound.

The single most important thing to grasp about the book of Jonah is that, whether or not it is history, it is a powerful parable, a parable whose intent is to shock and wound those to whom it is applied. *Jonah*, read aright, should come to us like a bolt of lightning to a sleeping man.

Our job, as we gather in the weeks ahead, will be to examine the book of Jonah and to watch its great themes come into focus. God's freedom and compassion, our deep prejudice and apathy toward those unlike us, the selfishness and disobedience of God's people, and the sign of Jonah as a Christ-type—all these will touch us and challenge us.

Discussion and Action

1. Sometimes first impressions are right on the mark. Other times they are way off base. But we have to start somewhere. Share your first impressions of Jonah with this in mind.

2. Clip cartoons from several newspapers or news magazines; find some that use humor to make a very serious point. Can you, as a group, agree about what is being said in each one? Discuss ways in which the humor is used to make the point more powerful than a simple statement of fact or opinion.

3. Are there instances in which humor is out of line or inappropriate? Would you agree with the author that the book of Jonah has a comic aspect? If so, share where you found humor.

4. All of us have felt burned by a teasing remark or a joke told at our expense. Have you ever been burned by a sermon illustration or a story or verse from the Bible? Recall what happened and how it affected you.

5. Read Job 5:17-18 and reflect on experiences of being God's wounded. Where is God in our experiences of pain and hurt?

6. Share the primary or central message of the book of Jonah for you and how it affected you. Perhaps, the message is a reminder about personal prejudice or an experience of having run away from God.

7. Close with a prayer that each one in your study group will be open to the message of Jonah in the weeks ahead.

2

Jonah ben Amittai
Jonah 1:1

Preparation

1. Reflect on both the benefits and dangers of nationalism. Think of Israel, America, and other countries. How does a zeal for unity and patriotic fervor help a country to survive, prosper, and provide a better way of life for its citizens? Think of times when such fervor has led to arrogance, oppression, or violence.
2. Read Psalm 137 and the book of Nahum. Try to imagine the suffering that must have prompted these cries. Think of how hard it would be to see God's grace going out toward those who inflicted such terrible pain on those you love.
3. The books of Ezra and Nehemiah describe what life was like for those who returned to Jerusalem after the exile; take some time to read parts of both Ezra and Nehemiah. Then consider how the book of Jonah might (if it were written at this time) have given the Jews a different perspective on Gentiles.

Understanding

Gorbachev, Gandhi, Picasso, and Paul. Jesus, Joan of Arc, and Jonah. All people. Fascinating, delightful, and astounding in turn. We want to know all about them. We want to know all about their times, their family, culture, religion, and the country that shaped their values and pushed them to their destiny. If we have to dig a long way into the past, as we do, for example, with Jesus, we discover that two or more personalities emerge: the person we want to study in the first place and the one who wrote about him.

When we read the Gospels, for example, we learn much about Christ. But there are four Gospels, and as we study them all, we also learn about their authors and the people to whom they wrote. We owe a great debt to scholars who study language and customs so that we can learn more about God's word and the people who received it first. Hearing it as they must have heard it helps us to interpret it aright for our own times.

There are two distinct persons who deserve our attention as we attempt to understand the book of Jonah: Jonah ben Amittai and the unnamed prophet who wrote his story many years later. Of the first, we know very little. It is clear from 2 Kings 14:25 that he was a real person who lived in the eighth century b.c. and prophesied in the reign of Jeroboam II. Although Jeroboam II was evil, Jonah prophesied that God would use his armies to save a weak and faltering Israel. The nation would recover the land which had been lost to Judah and other nations and expand her borders to boot.

The book of Jonah, which we now have, was probably written at least 400 years after Jeroboam II. By that time, the son of Amittai would have been reduced to a mere footnote in biblical history. While his prophecy was both faithful and correct, it pales beside the other prophets of eighth century b.c. After the kings Jeroboam and Uzziah died, the peace and prosperity foretold by Jonah were eclipsed by the utter darkness predicted by Amos, Hosea, Isaiah, and Micah. Yahweh, who had not ignored the evil of Israel and its kings, now used the kings of Assyria and Babylonia to chastise his people with war and defeat and captivity. Only after the terrible pain of exile did God return the children of Israel under the leadership of Ezra and Nehemiah to their land, bind their wounds, and restore their special identity as a covenant people.

Many scholars believe that it is at this point after the exile, while the wounds of war were still fresh and the humiliation of captivity was a stinging memory, that the book of Jonah was written. The author must have known of Ezra and Nehemiah and the tremendous effort they made as they led a group of bitter and broken people back to a destitute land. Some of the captives had forged a new life in captivity, marrying foreign wives, going into business, and experiencing the temptation to worship foreign gods. Ezra and Nehemiah had addressed this problem, in part, by preaching a fierce and uncompromising nationalism. Every man, woman, and child had to be focused on the goal of restoration. The word of God, the temple of God, and the people of God had to be rebuilt from the ground up if Israel was to survive as a nation. And in this political climate, it was easy for patriotic fervor to disintegrate into arrogant pride as well as a hatred of foreigners.

This is not to say that the author of Jonah worked against Ezra and Nehemiah or was opposed to their goals. But he saw that an Israel without a vision of a compassionate God, whose mercy would bless all nations of the earth, was headed for spiritual bankruptcy. He wanted to provide a corrective balance to postexilic nationalism the way we would apply a brace to a deformed foot. Without the brace, the child would be crippled. With it, the child could learn to walk straight.

To do this, the author of Jonah takes a real prophet about whom almost nothing is known (remember, 400 years have passed since Jeroboam II's reign) and makes him the central figure in a cunning parable designed to trap the listeners the way Jesus trapped the lawyer with the Good Samaritan. As soon as the author mentions Jonah ben Amittai, his hearers will begin to take the bait. You can almost feel the wheels turning as the audience swallows the first line. "Now the word of the Lord came unto Jonah the son of Amittai, saying . . . " We might try to imagine how the audience felt in those brief seconds before the scandalous mission to the cesspool of Nineveh is revealed. They must have said to themselves: "Jonah! In the time of Jeroboam II. Now there was a man, a real prophet of God. He came to us in the glory days before Amos and Isaiah came along with their messages of punishment and doom. Said we'd be great! Conquer the world! And we would have, too, if the stinking Assyrians had left us alone."

It must have been a real shock to hear, as radio commentator Paul Harvey says, "the rest of the story." Instead of being a hero, Jonah is a mess. Instead of predicting national expansion, he is sent to the capital city of the enemy. There is no doubt about it. The author's choice of Jonah ben Amittai (and of Nineveh, which was the capital city of Assyria) is a stroke of genius.

So then, two people emerge as we study the setting of the book of Jonah: the obscure prophet from the dim past and the author of this remarkable book. Both had a part to play in the history of God's people. The man whose name we remember prophesied a nationalism of power, conquest, and pride. The man whose name has been lost tells us that Israel's nationalism was secondary to her mission.

Understanding the setting for the book of Jonah helps us to apply the meaning of the text to our own situation. It helps us hear God's voice speaking to us about our own sinful attitudes as citizens in a nation that often regards itself as Christian. It forces us away from the pleasure of dwelling on our rights and privileges as a "chosen people" and points us to our responsibility to be a conduit or vessel for God's grace to all men and women and children (even beasts!), no matter what they believe or how they have acted in the past.

Discussion and Action

1.   What aspects of American government and life make you proud to salute the flag? Are there other aspects that inspire different feelings? Express these feelings to one another.

2.   What makes a nation "one nation under God"? Is it the faith of "the founding fathers"? The faith of current leadership? The fact that a majority of the citizens profess to be Christian? Fair and just treatment for all citizens under the law? Moral action in global affairs? Faithfulness to the gospel on the part of most (or even a remnant) of the people? Other criteria?

3.   On the basis of your answers above, do you think America can be considered a Christian nation? Why or why not?

4.   If the author of the book of Jonah were here, what do you think he would say to us about our attitudes toward countries such as Russia, Cuba, Israel, Iraq, and the Palestinian people?

5.   The repentance of the Ninevites and the impact of her change were both unbelievable and devastating to the prophet Jonah because he had to re-evaluate his prejudices and accept the unacceptable—that Ninevites were his brothers and sisters in the Lord. What changes will we have to make toward others as the Cold War grinds to a halt and former enemies abandon oppressive ways and turn toward peace?

6.   Are there individuals or nations that you consider beyond God's grace? Who are they, and why do you feel that way?

7.   Close the session by reading Jonah 4:11 aloud and praying for those you named and for each one in your study group.

3

What Makes Jonah Run?
Jonah 1:1-3

Preparation

1. Read Jonah 1:1-3 and Psalm 139:1-18. Spend time meditating on the truth that no matter where we go, God can find us. Remember times in your life when you were grateful for this reality and times when you would have appreciated a hiding place.
2. Jonah was not the only prophet to resist the call of God. Look up the call of other prophets and note the way they tried to evade responsibility: Moses (Exod. 3:7—4:17), Jeremiah (Jer. 1:4-10). What are their concerns? How does God reassure them?
3. Think of persons for whom and situations in which God is calling you to be a channel of grace. What tactics do you use to evade that call?

Understanding

The call of God upon Jonah is agonizingly clear and straightforward. Had it been less specific, less outrageous, who knows, Jonah might have tried to obey. As it is, his unqualified "No!" strikes a chord in all of us. The blunt refusal, coupled with a beeline in the opposite direction, has a childish, comic tone. Jonah will take his marbles and go home. The game is not to his liking. When we laugh at him, we are also laughing at ourselves.

The call of Jesus Christ upon our lives is no less outrageous. There are many specific commands in the New Testament that make going to Nineveh look like a cinch by comparison. Think about it. We are expected to love our enemies, to turn the other cheek, and to forgive without limits. Our lives are to be models of purity, compassion, and generosity to all. We're to be salt and light, in a word, "perfect," like our God. Our mission is not confined to one place, nor is it limited to one city or one pronouncement. God has not come down to us as individuals and requested one preposterous *thing*. Rather we are to live a lifestyle "worthy of the calling to which we have been called" (Eph. 4:1). Little wonder, then, that we sometimes want to go as far as possible from a God who demands nothing less than total commitment. It is an inner awareness of our own resistance to God's call that helps us appreciate Jonah's decisive action, even though we know that to resist is the wrong thing to do.

What is it about Nineveh that makes it a last straw for Jonah? Jacques Ellul, whose book *The Judgment of Jonah* (1971) is full of insight, helps us understand this point: "This people was a traditional foe of Israel. . . . Imagine a Frenchman going to preach repentance to Berlin in 1941 or 1942! [They were] the most martial, the most realistic, and the most cruel people of antiquity. It was the people who scorched its enemies alive to decorate its walls and pyramids with their skin" (p. 26).

In Jonah's eyes, Nineveh doesn't *deserve* the grace of God. In his mind, this city has already been tried, found guilty, and sentenced to die. All that remains for the Ninevites is to live out the remainder of their vile lives and check in at the gates of hell for their final reward. Jonah can't be bothered with the task of extending a warning to them, because Nineveh's destiny is a foregone conclusion in his mind. And so he runs.

We are invited, then, to ask, "What makes me run?" Is there a person, a nation, a group, a sin, an attitude, or a deed that I consider outside the realm of God's grace? Is there anyone or anything (including myself) that I've written off completely as either unworthy or impossible as a target for God's compassion and redeeming mercy?

The book of Jonah seems to be essentially about missions, about the need to evangelize and to warn others about God's judgment. But there is another factor here. Jonah runs not only from the task at hand but also from something larger and more threatening. Twice in these three verses, the author tells us that he is running *"from the presence of the Lord."* He books passage to Tarshish, not only to evade evangelism but to hide from his Maker. So we must also ask ourselves: What is it about God's presence that makes me want to play hide and seek?

What is it that God wants me to be or do (and it may have nothing whatever to do with missions) that I am resisting?

Jonah's action was direct and obvious. He got on a boat that was headed in the other direction. My own running may not be so obvious. I must ask myself where I am going in my relationships, in my work, in my church, in my community, in my devotional life, and in the world I share with others. Am I moving toward the Almighty or away from God? What kind of vessel carries me away from the Presence? Is it a lifestyle that is too busy? An ark of worries and anxieties? Destructive habits or addictions? A raft load of material things? Food, entertainment, or other pleasures that mask my real hunger for God? There are probably as many responses as there are persons.

Running is not simply an individual matter. Often, Jesus' parables were directed not at one individual per se but at community groups, such as the Pharisees. While they relished their identity as the chosen people, they avoided their obligations to the weaker members of the nation—the poor, the widows, the infirm, and the elderly (Matt. 23). The book of Jonah invites us to examine ourselves as a covenant community and to ask if we have been content with having the *name* of Christian (as the church of Sardis in Rev. 3:1) while fleeing from our responsibilities to the poor and oppressed. Do *we* make a show of worship as we run from our duty as stewards of this earth and from a genuine openness to the presence of the Lord?

As I write these words, it suddenly occurs to me that running from our Sovereign may not be, altogether, such a bad thing. It shows, after all, that we take God seriously and that we understand the implications of being caught. If I tell my young son that a great, invisible flesh-eating monster is even now at our door, ready to devour him, the boy will only laugh. He is certain that no such creature exists and that he will not be harmed or even disturbed. If I say, however, that I intend to chase him and tickle him or, in another vein, punish or discipline him, he may very well take to his heels. He understands that I am a real person with authority in his life and that when I speak to him in a certain way I mean business. Running implies both faith and respect on the part of the fugitive. It also implies that Someone cares enough to pursue.

All of scripture, the book of Jonah included, demonstrates that God is active when we run. We hide; God seeks. Francis Thompson says that God is the "Hound of Heaven" who follows us in hot pursuit. The Creator is present in the garden seeking the first couple as they cower among the trees. And the Creator is present, as well, in the prophet of Nathan as he confronts David with the terrible twin sins of murder and adultery. As a faithful husband in the guise of Hosea, God goes down to the slave market to buy back his faithless, runaway wife. God, as a mother bird, gathers the chicks under loving wings or, as a thrifty and determined wife, sweeps the house clean to search for a lost coin. As a loving father, God strains his eyes to see down the road where the Prodigal Son will come back into sight and goes running to meet him. Always, always, when men and women run, God pursues. And Jonah is about to discover that the boat has not been fashioned that will truly carry him away "from the presence of the Lord."

Jonah, of all people, might have known that there would be no safe haven on this cruise from the God of Israel. His flight is a farce! Surely the man of God and the prophet of the Most High will know that this is useless—yet he acts as though escape is an option! We see right away that it is not. Or do we? This book not only asks us to examine our own escape routes but to explore the roads that will lead us back to God.

Discussion and Action

1. Read aloud Jonah 1:1-3 and Psalm 139:1-18. Share with each other about times you have felt that you or someone close to you, "ran away" from God or literally ran away from home. Why did you or they run?

2. We know that Jonah ran because he was prejudiced against Nineveh. What constitutes a Nineveh for you?

3. What is God asking you to do or be that you may be running from right now?

4. From which specific tasks do you see the local church or the larger church running? How can your congregation help the denomination return to a closer walk with Christ and to obedience?

5. Make a commitment to one another in the weeks ahead to be accountable to one another about concerns for yourself, your congregation, the denomination, and the church at large.

6. Close with prayer, thanking the Hound of Heaven for seeking us out and bringing us home.

4

And Jonah Slept
Jonah 1:4-16

Preparation

1. Read Jonah 1:4-16 and Amos 6:1-7. What parallels do you see between Jonah's sleep and the complacency of those who feel secure in Zion?
2. Review the story of the Lost Son in Luke 15:11-35. How does God use the famine in this story and the storm in Jonah to motivate the central characters? Reflect on storms and times of famine in your own life that have moved you closer to God.
3. Make a list of non-Christians whom you have admired or learned from or who have had an important impact on your life. What qualities did they demonstrate that are pleasing to God? What characteristics of the sailors seem more godly than Jonah's? What does Jonah do that you *can* admire?

Understanding

Snoopy sits atop his doghouse and taps out a surefire beginning for an exciting tale: "It was a dark and stormy night." And with these words, he has our undivided attention. A storm, especially at sea, is a great setting for an adventure, because it speaks to all of us about the times in our lives of violent upheaval, of terror and uncertainty, of a crisis moment that will change our lives forever. Many great works of art and literature use the sea as a symbol for the world and the people aboard ship as types of characters in society; the book of Jonah is no exception. In many ancient stories, such as Shakespeare's *The Tempest*, audiences thought of storms as nature's reflection of the conflicts between the gods and people or between people or nations. The fate of the souls on a tiny ship in a moment of high drama becomes the destiny of us all.

Although it is brief, the scene here is vivid and charged with emotion. The fury of the wind and the violence of the storm threatened to dash the ship to pieces. We should feel, from this passage, not only the salt spray of the raging sea but also the fear and desperation of the sailors who do everything humanly possible to save the ship and their own lives. Their earnest prayers place them in direct contrast to our hero who, though he is the cause of this tempest, is ironically in the bottom of the boat sleeping like a baby.

These men are Gentiles—foreigners, pagans in Jonah's eyes— yet they seem to understand instinctively that this is not an ordinary squall. They cry out to their gods as though they understand what the author has clearly revealed to us: that the great wind and the mighty tempest are sent by Yahweh. Their vigorous action in throwing things overboard and in heartfelt prayer is comical when contrasted with Jonah's placid nap.

There is further irony and humor in their request that he pray so that his God "will spare us a thought so that we do not perish." Jonah has not escaped his mission! Even now, he must intervene or all of them, himself included, will die. It must have been a rude awakening, indeed, to hear on the lips of a pagan shipmaster the very words that God would have spoken in the flesh: "What do you mean, O Sleeper?"

Later on, in the belly of the fish, Jonah will have plenty of time to reflect on these ironies. Though he is stubborn and hardhearted about the Ninevites, the sailors are remarkably open and caring toward him as a person and determined to do the right thing. They patiently ask about his background and his reasons for running from God. Although they are terrified, they ask Jonah's opinion. (Most people I know would have lynched him first and asked questions later.) Even in the face of his response, they resist sending him to certain death. In trying to row ashore, they exhaust every possible appeal before applying the death sentence. Even then they pray and, as if to add insult to injury, offer a sacrifice to Yahweh and make vows. In every respect they are Jonah's spiritual superiors.

Jonah is praiseworthy in only two things. Here, as in the rest of the book, he maintains a dogged, blatant honesty both about his own feelings and about God. To the bitter end, like a mistaken umpire, he "calls 'em like he sees 'em." His only other asset (one we might have expected more from the sailors) is his courage.

This little section of Jonah is only twelve verses long, yet reading it is like watching a master artist who takes only a few deft strokes to create a scene of unusual power and complexity. The issues raised in this short drama are quite serious, despite the ironies and the air of comic melodrama. We might ask, for instance, what sort of God sends such a violent storm to work the divine will in a man's life (presumably at the possible expense of the sailors and others who might have perished had Jonah not confessed his crime). I have always suspected—though it is not stated—in the parable of the Lost Son that God allowed the famine which brought the boy to his senses. Here there is no guesswork. "The Lord hurled a great wind . . . " Nor is there much guesswork in the book of Amos (6:1-7) as God promises the complacent ones that the Lion of Judah will effect military ruin and exile on them for their lack of compassion. In Jonah, as in all of scripture, we see Yahweh as Sovereign over history. Over sweeping events such as the exile and the holocaust to the details which determine the fate of one tiny ship, Yahweh reigns.

And what sort of a fool, we might ask, could sleep in the face of such power and majesty? Where does a person who is so obviously important to God get the nerve to spit in the eye of the Almighty and the callousness to saw logs while his world is on the eve of destruction? Is he playing possum? Is he, so to speak, dead to the world?

And what of the sailors? How did the heathen come to care for the fate of one man? If they were merely inspired by the terror of dying, why did they resist casting Jonah into the sea? And why did they ask pardon, make sacrifice, and pay vows? How is it that, once out of danger, they did not dismiss the storm as coincidence and retire to a tavern for a drink and a yarn about their near miss, or return to their idols and thank *them*? How is it that these lost souls showed mercy and spiritual insight while the man of God remained closed to a whole city and deaf to the will of God?

All of these questions or issues about the sovereignty of God in history, about God's willingness to use or even initiate "storms" to accomplish the divine purpose, about our own slumber in the face of injustices, and about the irony of non-Christians who show moral courage and ethical insight are still alive today.

Jonah is a three-alarm fire, a jangling alarm clock, an unwelcome wake-up call for a covenant community which has been asleep on the job. While we can see small pockets of faithfulness in places such as South Africa and Central America, we are, for the most part, snoring on issues such as homelessness, poverty, hunger, and the environment. The rock bands and Hollywood stars who do concerts and benefits for AIDS and other pressing storms seem to me like the frantic sailors pitching cargo overboard to save the sinking ship of earth. Where is the church? Where are we? Wave after wave of disaster floods into our living rooms every evening on the news. It is no wonder that, like Jonah, we are overwhelmed by the notion that God's word has come to us, demanding, insisting that we wake up and do something about our responsibility for a world that clearly needs our help. What we'd really like to do is turn over and go back to sleep! It is Yahweh, like the shipmaster, who shakes us by the shoulders and forces us, along with the others who inhabit the good ship earth, to determine what it is we must do.

Study groups afford us a small measure of accountability. We can speak the truth to one another about the ways in which we have been purposely oblivious to God's call on our lives. We can challenge one another to wake up, to make and follow up on specific commitments. If we have questions about the way God works in the world or in nature or in political events, we can speak them here.

Discussion and Action

1. Share with one another about the "storms" or times of "famine" in your lives that God has allowed.
2. What questions and problems arise when we see *every* bit of suffering and disaster as coming from God's hand?
3. Who are persons outside the Christian faith who have had a significant impact on your lives?
4. How have we as individuals and as a church "been asleep" in the midst of injustice?
5. If anyone in the group has made a specific commitment as a response to God's call, listen to that person share his or her experience.

5

A Big Fish Swallowed Him
Jonah 1:17—2:10

Preparation

1. Read Jonah 1:17—2:10. Reflect on Jonah's experience in the belly of the big fish. Then put yourself in his place and think about what your response might have been. Would you have prayed the same kind of prayer as found in today's text? Why or why not?

2. Scan the story of Samson in Judges 13—16. Read the passage on his fall (16:16-22) and reflect on the time he spent grinding grain in the prison in Gaza. What must have been on his mind as his hair grew back? What parallels do you see between Jonah and Samson? What qualities of God come through as God uses these imperfect men?

3. Read one of the following: Psalms 88, 42, or 124. Reflect on the times in your own life when you have felt far away from God. Have you ever been cast down in depression or despair? What brought you down to "the pit"? People? Illness or death? Your own disobedience or sin? The loss of a friend? Was there a time when you felt unable or unwilling to pray? How did that change for you?

4. Use a Bible dictionary to find out about *Sheol* or the term *hades* or *hell*. When you read "the grave" or "the pit" in the Psalms, you are reading the translation for the Hebrew word *Sheol*. Be prepared to share your findings with the group.

Understanding

Some scriptures suffer neglect because of the baggage we bring
to them as we study, particularly in groups. The creation narratives are
a good example. It is such a temptation, as we gather, to debate about
evolution, creationism, myth, history, and so on, without even exam-
ining the text. We tend to have our minds made up about these
controversies, and we enjoy the lively discussions that flower forth
from them. Yet we may be missing out on the fruits. It is not so much
our opinions that matter, but God's message. Our passion to persuade
others about our point of view may divert us from the task of discerning
God's word.

Just as Jonah the prophet was swallowed by the fish, perhaps
Jonah the book has been devoured by our debates *about* the fish.
Seemingly, the book of Jonah suffers because of having become an acid
test for our views about the Bible. After all, if one can believe that
Jonah's life is a straightforward history, he or she is safe and secure in
the orthodox camp. Or it may be that one is liberal, proud to regard
Leviathan as a symbol, immune to jokes about the "fish story." Yet we
can be either of these without ever asking: What is the point? What is
the word of our God to the church in this hour? Together, we will turn
to this important question as we study Jonah's prayer from the maw of
this singular fish.

Whatever else we believe about this fish, we must accept that
(like the storm and, later, the plant, the worm, and the desert wind) it
was *appointed* by Yahweh to swallow the drowning man, to preserve
him alive, and to deposit him on dry land at last. This term *appointed*
—*minnah* in the Hebrew—means that it was ordained or commissioned
and placed by God in an intentional way. The term in the King James
Version makes it sound like God customized the beast to accommodate
a person. The fish, like the other aspects of nature and unlike Jonah
who rejected his ordination, is an obedient servant to God. We should
not envision the fish as a malevolent predator who adds to Jonah's perils
by attempting to eat him. The fish is just the opposite: a symbol of
grace, salvation, deliverance, and rescue. And the fish comes in the nick
of time, for the psalm in chapter two reveals that Jonah had been on his
way to Sheol, to "the uttermost parts of the sea" (Psa. 139 KJV).

Like King Midas of Greek mythology, Jonah, who wanted to flee
from the presence of the Lord, has been granted his wish, and it is not
to his liking. By sending the fish, God shows mercy to one who is both
undeserving and unrepentant. This act of amazing grace will be food

for thought in the three days to come. Jonah will be forced to think of Nineveh. Are the Ninevites really less deserving than he? Is deserving a factor at all? For now, though, he is glad to be delivered from the abyss.

From the moment that Jonah rebelled, he began a downward course that took him farther and farther from God, both in a spiritual and a literal sense. For the Hebrews, the place of the dead was below the earth, lower even than the depths of the sea. Our own language reflects this world view. We say, for example, "I'm really down," or "This job is the pits," or "It's been hell," or even "I'm a dead man." The Israelites saw depression, illness, abandonment, and other tragedies as death intruding into life. When Tamar was raped and scorned, for example, she mourned as though a death had taken place (2 Sam. 13:19). So did Job when he was stricken with boils (Job 2:8). Many psalms, including Jonah's prayer in chapter two, are packed with images of being swallowed, drowned, imprisoned, or trapped in the bowels of the earth. From the frying pan of Sheol, Jonah is swallowed into the belly of the fish. It is another kind of fire. Still a prison, still a pit, but now it is a place of preservation where he will be kept alive until he can do the only thing left *to* do: offer a prayer of thanksgiving from the belly of the fish.

The plight of Jonah echoes the agony of literally hundreds of men and women in the Bible. Jonah's prayer might have been the prayer of Eve after the fall, of Joseph in prison, of Jacob at Jabbok ford, of David as he ran from Saul, of Mary of Bethany as she mourned Lazarus, of Peter after the denial, of Jesus in the garden, and of his mother Mary as she held his broken body beneath the cross. These and many others knew what it was to be cast into the deep, to a place far from the face of God, a place where despair washes over the soul in relentless breakers, where the reality of death is a fierce undertow, and where the anguish of the spirit makes death seem quite welcome by comparison. We know, of course (from the safety of our armchairs), that God's presence reaches even to this place; but in the belly of the fish, a place of fear and guilt and doubt, that Face does not appear.

It must have been exceedingly difficult for Jonah to pray from that place. Like Samson grinding at the mill of the Philistines, Jonah knew beyond a shadow of a doubt that his own willful disobedience had brought him to this place. Why should God hear him at all? Again, we ask those questions of grace and mercy and *deserving*! And so it is that three days and nights pass before Jonah begins to pray.

It is significant to remember as the story of Jonah unfolds that this prayer is a psalm of thanksgiving rather than a lament psalm. Jonah is in the deep, dark belly of the fish, but he is alive, protected, and safe. He has been rescued by God through one of God's own creatures, a fish. Most scholars believe that the author of Jonah selected a well known psalm and inserted it word for word into the text. These may have been words that were said many times in prayer just as we might recall the 23rd Psalm in a time of crisis. But the images are especially suited to Jonah's plight. Now the images of a watery grave and terms like *belly* and *pit*—used so often for Sheol—take on new meaning as we picture the prophet in the innards of a fish, having been rescued literally from drowning. The promise at the end that "I will sacrifice to you; what I have vowed I will pay" surely means that Jonah will go to Nineveh at last.

When the last words of the psalm fade away, we move from the interior of the fish to the surface of the earth and the land of the living. Yahweh, ever sovereign, has only to speak to the fish. Gladly, the fish will disgorge its burden.

Unharmed, Jonah will "pay his vow," but the heart of the man remains the same. God can demand obedience, but even the Almighty cannot *command* compassion.

Discussion and Action

1. Read Jonah's psalm aloud. What psalms or other passages of scripture have been of special comfort to you in times of despair and sorrow?
2. Jonah and Samson removed themselves from the presence of God through deliberate sin. Are there other times when God seems far away?
3. Why does God go to such trouble to save and use people who seem to us to be so unworthy? Why doesn't the Almighty just find a more suitable vessel? What do your answers tell you about the nature of God in relationship to humankind?
4. If you've been "holding out" on God, this might be a good time to make a commitment that you've sensed God is calling you to make.
5. Before you go home, share what your week will be like in the land of the living.

6

Jonah Goes to Nineveh
Jonah 3:1-10

Preparation

1. Read Jonah 3. Ask yourself why Jonah went to Nineveh this time. Also, look for elements of surprise and irony.
2. What two specific things does Nineveh repent? What actions are taken as a sign of that repentance? If *your* hometown had been a victim of the Assyrian war machine, if you had been violated or lost possessions or had your home burned or lost a family member to the soldiers of this great power, would these actions of repentance have impressed you?
3. Reflect on your own feelings about apologies. Are there times when "I'm sorry" has not been enough for you? Is it easy or difficult for you to apologize to God? to others?

Understanding

Once upon a time there was a little boy who was ordered by his teacher to sit down. He firmly resisted but in the end, because the teacher was more powerful, the boy sat. And he said to her, "But inside I'm standing up!"

Jonah says nothing to God, but when the word of the Lord comes for the second time, he goes. A Sunday school teacher once asked ten-year-olds why they thought Jonah obeyed. Their answer was simple: "Same reason we obey our parents when they order us to clean our rooms. It's easier, less hassle. We *have* to!" Those students knew what all teachers and parents—including God, the ultimate parent—know: It is one thing to coerce or threaten or bribe children into doing what we want; it is quite another thing to create change in them, so that they value what we value and want what we want.

Jonah goes to Nineveh. On the outside, he is faithful the second time around. But for all of the eloquence of his psalm in chapter two, it is clear that his heart has not been changed by his experience at sea. His heart's desire is still that Nineveh should perish. (We see this in 4:5 when he sits to the east of the city. Traditionally, a blast of scorching desert wind would come from the east.) He loathes this city and its people. He loathes the fact that he must be the instrument of warning. He condenses the message into a mere eight words: "Yet forty days and Nineveh will be overthrown!" It is as if he has fashioned God's words of concern into a deadly sword. He will march through this town, plunge the knife home, and leave so he can watch them die.

It will be helpful in understanding Jonah if we try to imagine what it felt like for him to enter Nineveh and speak his piece. First of all, the sheer hugeness of the place is emphasized by the author. It is "exceedingly great" (v. 3), a city, three days journey in breadth. Commentators all agree that this is colossal by any ancient standards. Moreover, we should remember that in the initial call (1:2) Nineveh is "great" even to Almighty God! How must it have seemed to Jonah?

It is also colossal in terms of its wickedness. We should not have to try very hard to imagine the sort of evil and violence that must have greeted the prophet as he approached the outskirts of the city. Evidence of Nineveh's army may have reminded Jonah of rape, plunder, and destruction. Then, as now, the evidence of evil permeates the streets of a city with a visible, tangible force. There are pickpockets and prostitutes, corrupt officials and seedy taverns. Arguments arise from alleys and few venture out after dark. In contrast to the splendid buildings erected by the rich and powerful, the poor, the hungry, and homeless wander the streets. Jonah must have seemed like an Amish man, moving from the clean quiet farms of Lancaster County, Pennsylvania to the wealth and squalor of New York or Los Angeles. He is truly a stranger in the strange land of Nineveh. To fling his eight words on Nineveh must have felt like throwing a thimble of water on an inferno.

He walks for one whole day before stopping to speak. He must have expected ridicule and abuse, at the least. And, considering the success rate of the prophets in Israel, death may have been the least of his worries. The writer of the letter to the Hebrews notes that some of the prophets were "tortured.... Others suffered mocking and scourging ... chains and imprisonment. They were stoned, they were sawn in two

. . . destitute, afflicted, ill-treated . . . " (Heb. 11:35-37). *And this was in Israel!* What must Jonah have expected in this (as he wrongly judged) God-forsaken city? We do not know his thoughts, but we can easily guess that the response to his words came like a bolt from the blue.

His cry that they will have forty days is a standard biblical testing period, like the forty years in the wilderness or the forty days in the desert for Christ. It's like your dad who has come to the end of his rope, telling you that you have one semester to improve your grades or one hour to clean that rat's nest of a room or ten seconds to get your act together or you're going to be one sorry child. But Nineveh is not going to lose just privileges; she will be overthrown, a word that packs a wallop when you consider that it was used for Sodom. The wrath of the Chief Parent will be more like a nuclear blast than a trip to the woodshed. But Yahweh is the God of Israel, not of Nineveh. Jonah must have felt like a madman when he said those words, like a country preacher setting up a soapbox on Wall Street or skid row. What do *they* know of forty days or of Sodom's fate? But by now Jonah knows that there is no choice. And so, like a man who faces a tidal wave of rejection, he wades into the city, says his eight words to the deaf oceans of people, and waits to be swallowed by the incoming tide.

There is a tidal wave all right, but it is not the one he expected. With astonishing speed they believe, they fast, and they cry out to God. Everyone, from the poorest right up to the king, repents in dust and ashes. Moreover, (and this is a bitter irony in light of Jonah's stubborn judgmental attitude) they *understand* the merciful, loving intention that lurks behind the eight words. They fast and pray because they respect the freedom of God to change as we change. They sense in Jonah's God a commitment to compassion, and they act on it at once. Even the animals will be draped in sackcloth! It is as though the cows in the field know more about Yahweh than Jonah does.

The irony of Nineveh's repentance must not be lost on the church in this hour. The call of God on our lives to speak a word of grace to the nations has not been rescinded. A word of forgiveness, a word of reconciliation, a word of repentance, a word of love to Berlin and Dublin and Johannesburg and Moscow! Perhaps the men and women in cities like these know far more about the gospel message than we dare to imagine. It is almost certain that we know less than we think. We say we are a Christian nation, but the camera does not lie. Most nights, on the evening news, I think we look more like Nineveh than not. And some days, even the cows in the field seem godly in comparison to people, many of whom call themselves Christians. Nevertheless, for everyone—man, woman, child, beast—from the least to the greatest, the call to repentance is clear. If we but dare to speak it, the word of God will go forth and accomplish its purpose (Isa. 55:11), though we think it absurd and impossible.

Discussion and Action

1. Share with one another stories about people you've known who have totally surprised you with a major change for the better. What surprises have come about in the last few years on the political scene? Has the gospel been a factor in some of these changes? Name courageous men and women who have had a prophetic voice in bringing about change.

2. What does this mean: "His grace isn't cheap, but it's free"? Do you think Nineveh's repentance is based on cheap grace? What evidence in the text supports your response? Remember, anyone can put on a show for a few days.

3. One of the charges against Nineveh is violence. Physical violence, whether it is part of an act of war or not, is one of the most difficult things to forgive. Words of repentance do not seem to be enough. What occurs when we resort to "an eye for an eye"? What can we add to our words to bring about reconciliation?

4. Some might say that it's easy for God up there in heaven to forgive evil and violence. What has God done to demonstrate that divine forgiveness is not just cheap grace dispensed by One who knows nothing of suffering?

5. Name people and situations that seem like Nineveh to you at this time—hopeless and overwhelming. Consider actions you might add to your prayers that would help bring about forgiveness, love, repentance, or reconciliation. Then close by praying for the people or situations you have named.

7

But Jonah Was Displeased
Jonah 4:1-4

Preparation

1. Read Jonah 4:1-4. Then, review the parable of the Unequal Wages in Matthew 20:1-16. What is the point of the New Testament story? What does its theme have in common with the book of Jonah?

2. Read Romans 9:1-16. Reflect on God's treatment of Esau and others like him (Cain, for example, and the elder brother in the story of the Prodigal Son). Have you ever felt deep in your heart that some people were not treated fairly by God? That you were not treated fairly by God? Have you ever expressed such feelings to others? To God?

3. Think about the issue of fairness as it was applied in your home when you were growing up and, if you have children, how fairness applies now. What factors make it difficult to be perfectly fair to every child in every situation? Is there something we value even more than "perfect" fairness? Write down in one sentence what that is for you.

Understanding

The immediate, sincere, and complete repentance of Nineveh is an unpleasant shock to our hero. No less shocking to the reader is the discovery that Jonah is displeased with the success of his mission. He is not just miffed. He is *exceedingly* angry. For the first time since his psalm in chapter two (which was a formal prayer recited, as it were, under duress), he speaks to God in prayer. It is a very different prayer than the psalm. It is blunt. It is painfully honest. It is sullen. The tone of the prayer is both child-like and child-ish. It is childlike because it abandons the language of control and eloquence. This is not the plea of an intellectual who is spouting words to impress others. This is the raw cry of one who no longer cares what *anyone* thinks, God included. My own children speak to me in this tone when they have come to the end of their rope. They abandon all hypocrisy and forget the rewards of being obedient and submissive. They *will* be heard. They will speak the truth as they see it and take whatever consequences follow.

Perhaps we do not hear the childlike virtues of courage and honesty in the prayer because of the childish way in which it is spoken. It smacks of "I told you so!" and "See! See! I *knew* it would turn out like this and you'd let those rotten Ninevites live!" and then, with the melodramatic tone of a soap opera, "Why don't you just shoot me and be done with it!" There is a definite streak of humor here (tantrums are always amusing when they are happening to someone else), but it does not cancel out the elements of pain, fury, and bitter anguish.

Jonah's first request is that God hear his reason for running away in the first place. He knew all along the sort he was dealing with: merciful, gracious, slow to anger. (See Exod. 34:6-7.) It is as though Jonah is saying, "I knew the plot before I read the play. It's in the textbook. It's in the manual. It was taught me at my mother's knee. *Given* with the Ten Commandments on the tablets at Sinai! I could see what the ending was going to be, and I didn't want the part. I was not going to share center stage with Nineveh." The unspoken implication of this request is for God to understand that Jonah still considers the Ninevites ripe for judgment. A few days of mourning and some crocodile tears will not wash away the blood on their hands.

The second request is for a one-way exit visa from this twisted, insane world. Jonah very likely knew, or thought he knew, the second act of the play, and it is no more acceptable than the first. When all the excitement of the threat of doomsday dies down, Nineveh will return to the old ways of violence and evil. The memory of that emotional moment will fade, and Jonah will be remembered as the laughable little man who carried a sign: "Repent! The End of the World Is Near!" He will be a laughingstock in the eyes of his enemies. In the eyes of his fellow Israelites, Jonah will not only be eccentric—for who but a crazed man would carry a warning to Nineveh?—but maybe even a false prophet! After all, he said the city would be destroyed, and there it is!

His prayers, then, condemn God for being unfair both to Nineveh, for they deserve judgment, not mercy, and to Jonah, whose faithfulness will be rewarded with pain.

It is easy to laugh at Jonah only as long as we do not consider how much like him we are. It's a bit like looking in the warped mirrors at a fun house. It is fascinating and funny at first, but we soon grow weary of seeing our own features distorted. After a while we are anxious to be rid of those grotesque images and return to our own reassuring reflection in a normal mirror. But it is hard to shake the memory of those monsters in the fun house. We sing "Amazing Grace," but what we often long for is for fairness—the kind of fairness that guarantees judgment for our enemies (we can justify this by claiming that "they" are God's enemies, too) and mercy for ourselves.

If the parable of the Good Samaritan prompts us to ask "Who is my neighbor?" perhaps Jonah will move us to ask "Who is my enemy?" It is tempting to assert that we have no *real* enemies, but it hardly coincides with truth. Why else would Jesus command us to love our enemies (Matt. 5:44)? Or why would the psalmist be comforted by the presence of Yahweh as the host "in the presence of my enemies" (Psa. 23:5)? The history of individuals, nations, and denominations suggests that we not only have enemies, but we thrive on them. Our enemies differ according to our experience and belief system, but they do exist. Enemies tend to be faraway and different from us (communists or Muslims, for example, who are geographically or religiously different). Or enemies may be quite close, close enough to cause us pain and disappointment: like a parent, sibling, or child; like a boss, teammate, or co-worker; or sadly, like a member of the church.

All of this is complicated by the fact that there are real enemies to God. We are surrounded by violence, injustice, and disasters, and these are often excruciatingly unfair. We are expected, even commanded, to cry out. Why, then, is Jonah's prayer so silly in our eyes? The answer lies in the nature of grace.

Jonah's prayer leaves only two avenues: to kill the enemy or to finish him [Jonah] off. They both involve a solution which is the antithesis of grace: death. God wants something more than a city or a world or a prophet that is wasted. The dead are past redemption, past repentance, past restitution, past hope. Besides, the Noah story proves that God will only have to start over with the same raw material: us. And our history and our hearts tell us the same thing, that humanity is fatally flawed from the beginning. All of us stand in need of grace. And none of us deserves it.

Jonah's prayer tells us that he has not learned the fact that grace is always undeserved. I have seen brothers and sisters stand beside the bed of a dying parent and squabble in fury over possessions and money *which they have not earned and can never deserve*. They sound to me like Jonah: truly concerned, not with justice or fair play but, at heart, with selfish gain!

Jonah's question is not answered. Instead, God has a question for him. It is a question no less for us as we consider our enemies, those we despise and wish dead: "Do you do well to be angry?"

Discussion and Action

1. Share your prepared sentence about what parents value beyond the impossible goal of perfect fairness.
2. What seemed unfair to you as you were growing up? If you are a parent, what issues about fairness are important in your household?
3. Think of the globe as home to the human family, even animals, with God as the head or heavenly Parent. What strikes you as most unfair or unjust? What would you want to ask God if you could? Do you think you could speak your mind without fear of retribution—as Job did? Why or why not?
4. Who are your enemies? Have you ever, like Jonah, gone so far as to want them dead? Have you ever had an enemy who later became a friend?
5. When have you felt so humiliated that even death would have been welcome?
6. List two individuals or groups whom you do not understand or accept very well (because of disagreements or differences). Think of one step you could take toward each that would narrow the gap between you.
7. Join hands and make a circle. Close with prayer, giving each person in the circle an opportunity to express their particular concern or joy to God. Finally, pray the Lord's Prayer in unison.

8

I'd Rather Die Than Live
Jonah 4:5-11

Preparation

1. Read the Jonah text for this session and 1 Kings 19:1-18. Notice that both Elijah and Jonah have just come from successful missions yet, ironically, they wish to die. How does God both minister to and challenge Jonah and Elijah?
2. Write down your responses to the following questions and be prepared to share them with the group: What do you think Jonah was hoping for when he went outside the city? If the plant and the worm are an object lesson, what is the point?
3. When have you wept over something trivial or sentimental (like a sad movie)? When have you found your heart hard in the midst of a real tragedy?

Understanding

I heard a story once about the wife of an old Amish farmer. After years of complaining about her husband's long grey beard, the wife decided to force the issue. She waited until he was sound asleep and cut off half of the offending growth. Certain that he would shave the rest or at least discuss it with her (for he was the strong silent type), she could hardly wait till sunrise. Finally her humiliation would end. Imagine her surprise and shame when he rose the next morning only to go about his business without the slightest indication that anything had changed. He refused to acknowledge her action or be pressured by her outrageous trespass. It was *his* beard.

Jonah reminds me of the wife in this tale, and the farmer speaks to me of God. We would expect Jonah to return to his homeland and accept the salvation of Nineveh, but he does not. He insists that there will be a final scene to this farcical play, and he will be the star. He will not take this lying down. He hears God's question, "Do you do well to be angry?" and his answer is an unqualified "Yes!" When he stomps to the east of the city and sets up his booth, he says to God, "See! See this! I'm gonna sit here and wait till you blast this city to kingdom come!"

But, as the beard belongs to the farmer, so wrath and judgment and compassion and grace belong to God, not to us. If we are scandalized by the thing, so be it. We may pout and whine like the childish Jonah, but that's too bad.

We may threaten like a child who claims he will hold his breath "till I turn blue and die," but it's God's beard. And God is not as passive as the farmer. God will speak to Jonah in deed (through plant and worm and wind), and in word (with a final penetrating question).

We should think of the plant itself as a *super* natural phenomenon. An ordinary feature of nature, like storms and fish, the plant is ordained or appointed to step out of its ordinary role and respond to God's sovereign command. The plant, like the fish, is an instrument of salvation and deliverance. It saves Jonah from the heat of the noonday sun as the fish saved him from death in the sea. It is also a sign to Jonah that, despite his early disobedience and his ill will towards Nineveh, God still cares enough about him to meet his needs. As the angel was sent to Elijah with nourishment and water, the plant is sent to Jonah. Providentially, it wraps itself around the makeshift booth and shields his body from the elements.

For Jonah, who may have expected to die at his own request, it is nothing less than a miracle. It is the voice of God saying, "I don't want you to die, I want you to live." Its sudden appearance is not ordinary, but *extra* ordinary, and makes Jonah exceedingly glad (v. 6a). Perhaps Jonah thinks that, like Jacob, he has wrestled with God and prevailed, or like Elijah, he has asked to die and been refused. Perhaps, as Elijah lived to see the gory death of Ahab and his wife, Jonah imagines that he will be permitted to witness the fiery death of Nineveh. Who knows? He may even go on to do great things in Israel and, in the end, be swept up into heaven and not taste death!

It is not certain that Jonah envisioned all these things. What *is* certain is that he has placed himself on a par with Elijah and that the plant is a sign of God's favor. But Jonah is no Elijah. And God, who takes no pleasure in the death of the wicked, has not saved this peevish prophet so he can indulge in base revenge. Rather, in this tale of strange reversals, there will be one more surprise.

The final twist comes in a one-two punch. The worm and the wind provide the prophet with a small taste of his own medicine. Not fire and brimstone, but a scorching east wind. Not enough to kill, but enough to make one wish to die.

Jonah's final request is brushed aside. And God, whose patient tender probing stands in direct contrast to Jonah's bitter rage, asks the final poignant question: "You pity the plant . . . should I not pity Nineveh?" This question ranks with the questions of Jesus in his parables. The sound of it should ring in our hearts as the sound of the pure, perfect pitch of the tuning fork, against which all sounds and tones are measured. This note of divine love and compassion reverberates through centuries of human prejudice and pride. It has, thank God, no end.

In the vastness of Nineveh, we should see the world in its complexity. Even with its history of violence and evil, it holds the potential for repentance and redemption. In the 120,000 we should see our neighbors, near and far, who have not known Christ and who stumble in the dark, not knowing truth from falsehood or good from evil. The analogy of the plant implies that God has tenderly nurtured each of these lost souls and labors over each one daily, hoping against hope for signs of life, growth, and health where there has been, up to now, only blight. And in Jonah, sad to say, we should see ourselves.

The darkness of Jonah's thirst for revenge is not as far away as we might like to think. Our eyes are accustomed to it. The darkness is present as we debate capital punishment. It cheers the electric chair and the gas chamber as a modern-day brimstone on people who are, to us, like Sodom. Few will intervene on their behalf, as Abraham intervened on behalf of Sodom.

When our armies avenge the insults and crimes of those we call our enemies, the Jonah-darkness blinds us to the pain of the innocents caught in the crossfire.

The Jonah-heart, a heart of darkness, tells us that people are somehow expendable in the grand scheme of things if they do not share our values, if they are impoverished, or if their beliefs or racial status are different from ours. If people are homeless or poor or addicted to destructive behaviors or destructive substances or are mentally ill or imprisoned or dying of AIDS, the heart of Jonah will speak: "Let them suffer. Let them die! They have brought this on themselves."

The language of Jonah is the language of *we* and *they*. It assumes the righteousness of the speaker and the capital guilt of *those other* people. Never mind that God's mercy has rescued us from the depths of the sea or that children (this may be the meaning of those who "do not know their right hand from their left" in 4:11) will suffer with sinners. The voice of Jonah cries out for a form of justice that knows pity only for *me* and *mine*.

Above the voice of Jonah, above his stingy heart, far above his ridiculous antics are another Voice and another Heart that continue to speak and to act. It is a Voice that is active, sovereign, persistent, and powerful. It is not a pre-recorded Voice, because it comes forth from a compassionate and responsive Heart, not from a book of laws that will mete out blind justice according to predetermined rules.

The Heart, of course, belongs to Yahweh, Creator not only of those who belong to Israel and to the church, but also of *all* men, women, children, even animals that exist on this planet. Intolerant of violence and evil, it is a Heart that is ablaze with mercy, patience, tenderness, and love.

Discussion

1. Read aloud 1 Kings 19:1-18 and Jonah 4. Share your comparisons of Elijah and Jonah. How does God minister to and challenge them?
2. Discuss the questions raised in the Preparation section, question 2.
3. Discuss the following statement: "All of this love and forgiveness is fine and good, but it doesn't take into account the pain of the victims and neither does the book of Jonah. The message of Jonah is simply not practical for our time."
4. Explore options for action that take into account both the victims and the offenders.
5. Covenant to research what could be done to respond with compassion to AIDS victims or drug users in your community.
6. Talk about the Heart and the Voice that are Yahweh's, the Creator's. How do you know that this compassionate and responsive God touches your life?

9

Parable of Forgiveness
Matthew 18:23-35

Preparation

1. Read the text for today's session. Then, reflect on God's compassion and forgiveness. List the similarities between this parable and the story of Jonah.
2. Reflect on the importance of forgiveness in the following scriptures: Matthew 5:7; Matthew 6:12-15; Matthew 19:27-30 and 20:1-16. Note that in the first two references our own forgiveness is possible *only if* we forgive others.
3. Read James 5:14-16 and reflect on the effect of unforgiveness on the person who withholds pardon from another.
4. Think about a time or times in your own life when you desperately needed to be forgiven by God or someone else. Did you or did you not experience forgiveness? What did that forgiveness or lack of it mean to you then and now? Reflect also on one or two times when it was difficult for *you* to forgive someone else.

Understanding

While our first eight sessions focused directly on the book of Jonah in the Old Testament, our last two will take us to the book of Matthew, where we will see how Jesus uses the theme of forgiveness in his teachings. The final lesson will examine Jesus' only direct reference to the story of Jonah and explore the meaning of the "sign of Jonah" for our time.

As we move into the study of the New Testament, we would do well to set aside the popular but mistaken notion that we have two separate and different Gods in addition to the two covenants. Looking at the book of Jonah and the parables of the kingdom is a perfect way to counter the myth that God of the Old Testament is a fierce, harsh God of unforgiving judgment, while Jesus presents a watered-down version of a God who dispenses "love" and cheap grace without concern for justice or any sense of mercy and compassion for the oppressed.

Rather, in the book of Jonah, we have a portrait of God who (although sensitive to the wrongs of Nineveh and willing to chastise both the city and the unforgiving prophet) is surprisingly tender, patient, and gracious. As we look at the teachings of Jesus, we will see that a similar portrait of God emerges. The one who is both fully human and completely divine clearly teaches that judgment is inevitable for the "sons of the evil one" (Matt. 13:42) and that mercy for the faithful is contingent on their willingness to forgive others "from the heart" (Matt. 18:34-35). It is of utmost importance that we, as sons and daughters of the new covenant, recognize that the terrors of divine judgment and the responsibilities of covenant mercy belong not only to a faraway God in the distant past but to us as well.

The story of Jonah and the parable of the Unforgiving Servant have an obvious common theme: that the mercy and compassion of God are available to all who ask pardon and truly repent. But there are other more subtle similarities as well. The enormity of the debt of the servant and the sins of Nineveh pose a serious theological problem. God, like the father in the parable of the Prodigal Son, looks like a fool. Who could forgive such an outrage? Worse yet, God seems unfair. This was supposed to be a day of accounting (Matt. 18:23). Instead, it is turned into a day of pardon. Grace, considering the crime, seems like an outrage. As it was for the prodigal's elder brother, grace is obscene (as opposed to being merely amazing). These elements—grace that's a scandal or outrage and pardon that smacks of injustice—appear in the parable of the Unequal Wages as well (Matt. 20:1-16). Every single one of these stories is trying to speak to human objections to divine grace.

Then, too, there are similarities between the character of Jonah and the character of the servant. If God's grace is outrageous, then their actions are infinitely *more* outrageous. Each man is eager to receive God's gracious gifts as long as those gifts are lavished on self. Jonah is glad for the fish and overjoyed for the plant because they are signs of God's deliverance and mercy. God forgives his deliberate disobedience and stubborn prejudice but, to the bitter end, Jonah cannot forgive

Nineveh. The servant is also eager to embrace outrageous grace as long as it serves his own ends. But, when the tables are turned, the servant cannot forgive his fellow servant. The staggering amount of his debt, in contrast to the pittance owed by the other servant, serves to show how stingy he is in comparison to God. Jonah, too (in addition to being childish), is miserly with mercy when it comes to Nineveh. Like Scrooge hoarding gold, he hoards grace for himself and denies it to other human beings.

This utter selfishness, this shocking ugliness shown by Jonah and the wicked servant, makes God's grace shine like the sunrise by comparison. When we see Jonah sitting up on that hill, hoping for Nineveh's incineration, and one servant allowing the other servant to be dragged off to prison, any doubts we may have had about the questionable nature of God's grace evaporate like dew in the sun.

Although both stories emphasize grace and have similar main characters, there are differences. The Jonah narrative is more complex and is full of sensational events and ironic plot twists. And, although the book of Jonah packs a prophetic punch, it also has an element of humor that is absent in the parable of the Unforgiving Servant.

But the New Testament parable, along with many other teachings of Christ on forgiveness, pushes us beyond the book of Jonah in some significant ways.

The astronomical size of the debt owed by the wicked servant helps us realize how different God's value system is from our own. For us, there is a kind of "scale" for sins, with some offenses more serious (and demanding more severe penalties) than others. But the horror of *all* sin and the holiness of God reveal that we have all incurred a debt to God which is utterly impossible to pay. Through the cross we have had that debt removed. *How dare we*, then, refuse to forgive our brothers and sisters?

This brings us to another crucial difference. Jonah's story is about forgiveness for those outside the faith. But the parable of the Unforgiving Servant acknowledges the fact that, for many of us, the most difficult people to forgive are those closest to us biologically, geographically, and spiritually. Jesus told this parable in response to Peter who wanted to know how many times he had to go on forgiving *his brother*.

Also, with Jonah, we are not told whether he learns from his adventures. God's final question is left hanging in the air so as to pierce the hearts of the listeners. But the fate of the wicked servant is terrifyingly clear. He will suffer as he wanted the other servant to suffer. Unlike Jonah, who received grace despite his unwillingness to forgive the Ninevites, the overwhelming debt of the servant will stand. Grace will be denied, and he will receive the maximum sentence because he did not forgive his brother. This appalling fact—that God's mercy to us depends on our treatment of others—is echoed in the Beatitudes and in the Lord's Prayer.

Shakespeare once said that the quality of mercy is twice blest; it blesses the one who gives and the one who receives. But the bitter little man on the hill and the wretched wicked fool rotting in a debtor's prison teach us that the reverse is also true. Failure to forgive is a double-barreled curse. It is a burden to the one who needs forgiveness and deadly torment to the one who withholds it. James 5:13-16 suggests that people suffer, sicken, and die without forgiveness, and Jesus indicates in this parable that those who don't forgive will find life hell if not in this world, then certainly in the next.

Discussion and Action

1. Share your reflections on God's compassion and forgiveness from your preparation. Then compare your lists of similarities between the parable of the Wicked Servant and the story of Jonah.
2. If God accepts "deathbed conversions," why would anyone accept the struggle and self-denial necessary to be a disciple? Why would God allow someone to sneak in by the back door at the eleventh hour (Matt. 20:1-16)?
3. When have you experienced genuine forgiveness from another Christian when you needed it most? What impact has that had on your life?
4. Why is it that we have the most trouble offering forgiveness to those close to us? When have you had trouble forgiving? What helped you set aside your anger and thirst for retribution and move toward forgiveness?
5. How can unconfessed or unforgiven sins have an adverse affect on our emotional, spiritual, and physical health? How can unforgiveness hurt the one who refuses to pardon a brother or sister?
6. Close with prayer and, if needed or desired, make commitments to seek forgiveness, reconciliation, and healing.

10

The Sign of Jonah
Matthew 12:38-42

Preparation

1. Read today's text and the following passages to determine the meaning of the term *sign*: Exodus 4:1-9; Luke 16:19-31; Luke 23:8-11; John 6:25-35; Matthew 24:24-27; John 20:24-30. Why and how are signs given?
2. Read Matthew 7:9-11 and Mark 2:23-28. Notice the logic of Jesus' argument. He moves from a clear, obvious, *accepted* conclusion (using "how much more") to make a point for the case at hand. Now read Matthew 12:38-42 to see how this same logic is used to compare Jonah with Jesus and Nineveh with the generation who lived at the time of Jesus.
3. In 1 Peter 3:8 the Apostle calls the brethren to unity and love in the face of coming persecution. Read 3:18-22 to see what Jesus did "in the heart of the earth" and what his example and resurrection mean for the church then and now.

Understanding

As we saw in our study last week, the message of the book of Jonah is echoed again and again in the teachings of Christ. To conclude our study, we will examine the only New Testament text in which Jesus' resurrection is linked to Jonah's emergence from the belly of the "whale." (Matthew's word *ketos*, meaning sea monster, is translated "whale" in many versions, leading generations to picture and speak of "Jonah and the whale.")

Wherever Jonah is mentioned, the enemies of Christ come asking for a sign. Twice in Matthew's Gospel (also Matt. 16:1-4) and once in

Luke (11:29-32) Jesus refers to Jonah as a response to those who would demand a sign. The impression is that Jesus was often, if not constantly, badgered for signs, both by the crowds (John 6:30) and by the crafty temple leaders. Thus we would do well to consider what is packed into the word *semeion*, or sign.

Signs and wonders have a rich history in both testaments, beginning with Moses and continuing with the Apostles (Acts 5:12). The latter chapters of the book of Revelation promise that, even at the end of history, "great signs" (Rev. 13:13-14) will be performed—in this case, false signs given by the beast—to convince the masses that divine power and authority accompany the words of a prophet or leader.

The word *semeion*, along with *dunamis*, from which we get our words dynamo and dynamite, is usually translated "miracle." These include (among other things) healings, exorcisms, the miraculous provision of bread, and, of course, the raising of the dead. All of these things are most impressive but, sad to say, often do not accomplish what we might expect: faith, repentance, and a life conformed to the will of God. Pharaoh, for example, was bombarded with signs but didn't move to free the slaves until his son was taken. Even then he sent soldiers to take the Hebrews back! The children of Israel, who were given the parting of the Red Sea, manna, water, and so on, continued to doubt, rebel, and sin against God. When they did respond to signs and wonders, their interest tended to be short-lived. (Psalm 78 is a long catalog of God's signs and Israel's rebellion).

John's Gospel makes it especially clear that Jesus had no intention of being a kind of spiritual Houdini. His works were not going to be mere displays of celestial clout to gratify whims, assuage hunger pangs, or startle and amaze the crowds. They were markers, indicators, divine "one way" *signs* intended to point from Jesus to the Father or to something of eternal importance. In raising Lazarus, for example, Jesus returns his friend to Mary and Martha in an incredible act of power. But it is more than a miracle or even an act of compassion. It is a *sign* that "I am the resurrection and the life."

What, then, is the sign of Jonah? As far as being wonderful or miraculous, it is no sign at all. It's as if a teen-aged boy came to his father and said, "Dad, I want to lift weights," intending for the father to buy an expensive, unnecessary set of weights. "You wanna lift weights?" the father replies. "Then take out the trash." The sign of Jonah is not quite what the scribes and Pharisees had in mind.

Nevertheless, the sign of Jonah is a real sign. It points to two things. First, it points to the sinfulness of those who are asking for wonderworks or "proofs" of Jesus' ministry *when they don't have the slightest intention of trusting him or repenting of their sins*. These evil men are not open to God or to the precious Child whom God sent. They may not be adulterers cheating on their wives, but they are unfaithful to God, rejecting the Messiah and opting, instead, for the false gods of status, power, and spiritual pride.

The sign of Jonah points the finger of condemnation at all those who have heard the preaching of Jesus and could have listened to the wisdom of his words and still reject him, refusing to believe and repent. This first sign is full of a bitter irony. A pagan queen and a heathen nation will rise up and condemn these pious religious leaders. Why? Because if Nineveh could repent after only eight words from the likes of Jonah, *how much more* should these "pillars of the faith" repent at Jesus' preaching? And if the queen of Sheba came from the ends of the earth to hear Solomon, *how much more* should these children of Israel hear (and believe) the Christ of God so close at hand?

The sign of Jonah points to a second truth as well. It points to the glorious resurrection of Christ after his descent into the heart of the earth. Matthew, who wrote his Gospel account for a Jewish Christian community of believers, is the only Gospel writer to see a prophetic prediction of the resurrection in Jesus' reference to Jonah. His readers, who would know the story of Jonah so well, would immediately catch the irony and contrast so evident in comparing Jonah and Jesus.

Jonah was headed for Sheol because he was disobedient. Jesus, on the other hand, led a life of perfect obedience. Jonah refused to head for Nineveh till he was forced, but Jesus willingly set his face for Jerusalem, knowing that the cross would await him there. Jonah sat in the belly of the fish for three days and nights before he could bring himself to pray. Jesus, Peter tells us (1 Pet. 3:19-20), spent his time below preaching to those who had lived and died before his time—even to those who had disobeyed God in Noah's time—so that not one soul would be lost. What compassion! What love! Finally, Jonah was vomited up—a distasteful meal, enough to give a whale indigestion—whereas Jesus, in the ultimate sign of God's power and glory, rose from the dead on Easter morn and lives forevermore. Although those scribes and Pharisees could not have known it then, the sign of Jonah as a prediction of Easter is the most awesome sign of God's power, triumph, and glory known to humankind.

None of the signs which Jesus did were for the exclusive benefit of those at hand. The miracle of the loaves in John 6 did not merely feed a hungry crowd for one meal for one day. It is a sign for all of us in this hour, a sign which points us to the fact that, if we don't partake of Jesus' flesh and blood and live in obedience and communion with him and with his body, *we have no life in us.*

The sign of Jonah is also a word for us today. If we do not abandon other gods and repent of our sin, we will be condemned along with those from previous generations. After all, we have the New Testament, the Spirit, and the gifts. We know the truth of the resurrection.

But the sign of Jonah is also a word of hope. The same God, who spoke to the rebel prophet on behalf of a pagan city and who sent Christ to die for us, also raised him from the dead and sends us in his name, through the Spirit, into the world to tell of God's love and mercy and compassion for all.

As I write these words, it is spring, and the evidence of new life is everywhere. Easter is fresh in my mind, and Christ's death and resurrection are quite real. Perhaps you will read these words when the shadow of death is real, in the earth or in your soul. May the sign of Jonah come to you as bread comes to a starving child, as living water comes to a thirsty soul. For the sign of Jonah comes to us in the depths of Sheol and says, "I raised Christ from the dead; I can lift you up, even from here."

Discussion and Action

1. Reflect on the meaning of signs in a scientific, skeptical, and materialistic age.
2. The sign of Jonah has two words: a word of warning and a word of hope. What do these mean for you today?
3. If Jesus were here, what do you think he would say about "this generation"? Who are our "scribes and Pharisees"?
4. Share with each other what the reality of the resurrection has meant to you over the years.
5. Sum up the main points of the book of Jonah. What one thing has come through for each member of the group that has touched or challenged you most?